●═ MASTERING CHANGE MANAGEMENT

A Practical Guide To Turning Obstacles Into Opportunities

Richard Y. Chang

Richard Chang Associates, Inc.
Publications Division
Irvine, California

MASTERING CHANGE MANAGEMENT

A Practical Guide To Turning Obstacles Into Opportunities

Richard Y. Chang

Library of Congress Catalog Card Number
93-74767

© 1994, Richard Chang Associates, Inc.
Printed in the United States of America

ISBN 1-883553-54-7
Second printing August 1994

Richard Chang Associates, Inc.
Publications Division
41 Corporate Park, Suite 230
Irvine, CA 92714
(800) 756-8096 • Fax (714) 756-0853

RICHARD
CHANG
ASSOCIATES

ACKNOWLEDGMENTS

About The Author

Richard Y. Chang is President and CEO of Richard Chang Associates, Inc., a diversified organizational improvement consulting firm based in Irvine, California. He is internationally recognized for his management strategy, quality improvement, organization development, customer satisfaction, and human resource development expertise.

The author would like to acknowledge the support of the entire team of professionals at Richard Chang Associates, Inc., for their contribution to the guidebook development process. In addition, special thanks are extended to the many client organizations who have helped us shape the practical ideas and proven methods shared in this guidebook.

Additional Credits

Editors:	Scott Rimmer and Sarah Ortlieb Fraser
Reviewers:	Pamela Wade, Ruth Stingley, and Joe Wilson
Graphic Layout:	Suzanne Jamieson
Cover Design:	John Odam Design Associates

PREFACE

The 1990's have already presented individuals and organizations with some very difficult challenges to face and overcome. So who will have the advantage as we move toward the year 2000 and beyond?

The advantage will belong to those with a commitment to continuous learning. Whether on an individual basis or as an entire organization, one key ingredient to building a continuous learning environment is *The Practical Guidebook Collection* brought to you by the Publications Division of Richard Chang Associates, Inc.

After understanding the future *"learning needs"* expressed by our clients and other potential customers, we are pleased to publish *The Practical Guidebook Collection*. These guidebooks are designed to provide you with proven, *"real-world"* tips, tools, and techniques on a wide range of subjects that you can apply in the workplace and/or on a personal level immediately!

Once you've had a chance to benefit from *The Practical Guidebook Collection*, please feel free to share your feedback with us. Your feedback is so important that we've included a brief *Evaluation and Feedback Form* at the end of the guidebook that you may fax to us at (714) 756-0853.

With your feedback, we can continuously improve the resources we are providing through the Publications Division of Richard Chang Associates, Inc.

Wishing you successful reading,

Richard Y. Chang
President and CEO
Richard Chang Associates, Inc.

TABLE OF CONTENTS

1. **Introduction** 1
   Why Read This Guidebook?
   Who Should Read This Guidebook?
   When And How To Use It

2. **Change Can Be Managed** 5
   Who's Behind Your Change?
   What's Behind Your Change?
   Who Makes It Happen?
   What Changes Can Be Managed?

3. **The Six-Step Change Process** 13
   A Model For Managed Change

4. **Step One: Clarify Your Need** 17
   Why Change?

5. **Step Two: Define Your Results** 29
   Decide On Your Desired Outcome
   Determine Its Feasibility
   Consider Its Evaluation
   Recognize Who Will Be Affected

6. **Step Three: Produce Your Plan** 39
   Analyze The Impacts And Requirements
   Organize Your Change Plan

7. **Step Four: Implement Your Plan** 59
   Monitor Your Action Plan
   Communicate Progress
   Determine And Communicate Any Changes To Your Action Plan
   Report Your Overall Progress
   Adjust Targets

8. **Step Five: Stabilize Your Outcome** 69
   Communicate That The Desired Outcome Is Now In Place
   Provide Recognition For Those Who Supported The Change

9. Step Six: Assess The Process 75

Issues To Consider

10. Encouraging Commitment To Change 89

Attitudes About Change
Steps To Overcoming Resistance
Attitudes Influence Behaviors
Obstacles To Opportunities

11. Summary 103

Appendix: Reproducible Forms 105

CHAPTER ONE

INTRODUCTION

Why Read This Guidebook?

Change is no longer a choice. It has railroaded its way over all organizations, impacting CEOs, middle managers, and entry-level employees alike. Chances are you've been hit by change in your organization.

You know its impact. Poorly managed change is confusing at best and counterproductive at worst. It makes you cringe. It causes anxiety. It creates chaos.

But you do have a choice in the matter. Given the task of tackling change, you can choose either to build an obstacle or to capitalize on an opportunity.

This guidebook enables you to gain control over change. It will lead you through the steps of effective change management and help you produce the results you want. If you desire to master change management, this guidebook will show you how to become an engineer of change.

Who Should Read This Guidebook?

Anyone in an organization who is or will be involved in planning, introducing, implementing, and managing change (*managers, supervisors, individuals tasked with being "change agents," team leaders, etc.*) will benefit from this guidebook. If you are not directly involved in managing change, but will be affected by it, there are sections in this guidebook that will prove valuable to you as well.

And, if you are just contemplating change, this guidebook can help you clarify your goals. Thus, if you have any stake in the change process you should read this guidebook. It could mean the difference between creating turmoil and moving successfully toward the desired state of change.

When And How To Use It

Use the tips and techniques in this guidebook before, during, and after change affects your organization. When you are planning for change, thoroughly consider all the questions and options discussed in this guidebook to help you choose the most effective course to take.

In the midst of change, *Mastering Change Management* will teach you how to deal with resistance. And once change has been implemented, you'll discover how to evaluate the change process— a crucial step in achieving even greater success the next time.

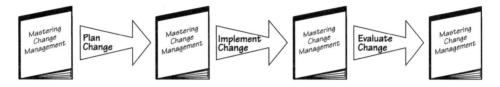

The six-step change model used in this guidebook may be perfect for your organization. On the other hand, you may find that you need to adapt it to fit your particular situation.

In addition, you may wish to consider combining the six-step model *(which looks at change from a systematic, or "big picture" perspective)* with the model presented in Chapter Ten, which focuses on the human element in the change process.

An ideal scenario may be for you to begin working through the six-step model, and then *"exit"* to the more specific model for overcoming resistance in Chapter Ten *(when you need to address specific instances of resistance to the change process)*. Then move back into the six-step model and put your change back on track.

Note: *Mastering Change Management* utilizes effective problem-solving tools that are more fully discussed in other books in The Practical Guidebook Collection, such as *Step-By-Step Problem Solving*, or *Continuous Improvement Tools*, Volumes 1 and 2. In addition, you may find it helpful to use the companion video, *"Mastering Change Management."*

CHANGE CAN BE MANAGED

Organizations continually evolve; whether by expanding, contracting, exploring, or eliminating. Managers often joke that change is the one constant in any organization, and it's undeniably true. Any organization that desires to improve or just keep up with its competitors has to change. People like you are often caught in the middle. You're probably responsible for planning, implementing, and ensuring that any change is successful. That's stressful!

Step One: Clarify Your Need
Step Two: Define Your Results
Step Three: Produce Your Plan
Step Four: Implement Your Plan
Step Five: Stabilize Your Outcome
Step Six: Assess The Process

Managing change is not easy, but you can do it, and you can do it well. Following a change management process will relieve some of your stress. In fact, it may be your lifesaver. By managing change effectively, you'll control change instead of letting it control you.

Who's Behind Your Change?

You currently may or may not be pushing for a particular change in your organization. Perhaps the top decision makers have decided a change is in order. Maybe one of your employees has suggested a change that could improve productivity. Or maybe you've identified an innovation and are eager to start the change process.

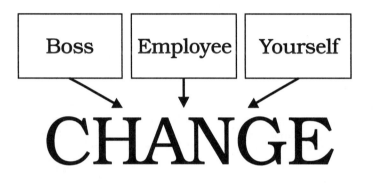

Regardless of who's behind your change, its success or failure depends on you. Manage the change successfully, and you'll have a great accomplishment to your credit. More importantly, you'll have the confidence to continue harnessing the power of change, and your employees will be more receptive to change the next time.

What's Behind Your Change?

What's motivating the change you'll be making? Do you have outdated equipment that needs replacing? Most organizations are motivated to make that change at some point. Or . . .

➠ Perhaps your product line needs an overhaul to boost sales. For example, a major toy manufacturer regained its market share after the head of the company decided to dump all products geared for children over the age of six. The company switched its focus to develop toys only for younger kids.

➠ Maybe the economy necessitates streamlining a process. One major consumer products company recently streamlined many of its work processes in an effort to increase profitability.

➠ Could it be that your customers have changed their needs and expectations? Witness a major auto manufacturer's goal to produce less expensive cars and join the minivan market.

➠ Perhaps a prevailing attitude needs adjusting. A major fast-food franchiser had to change to become more receptive to both its customers and its franchisees. As a result, the franchiser slashed prices and lowered restrictions on the franchisees abroad who wanted to market different menu items.

Understanding what's behind your change will move you and your employees ahead in mastering the change process.

Who Makes It Happen?

Contrary to popular belief, *"decrees from the top"* aren't the reasons for successful changes. A CEO might demand change, but it's the managers, the *"change team,"* and the employees affected by the change who make it happen.

WIN — WIN

You greatly increase your chances of a productive change by establishing a proactive change team. The active involvement of your team members will put you ahead of the game. A team can touch more bases than any one individual; and, if managed well, your team will be able to elicit more support for the change from other employees, resulting in a *"win-win"* situation.

What Changes Can Be Managed?

Just as any sports team needs a manager to help it reach its goals, change also requires management. It doesn't matter whether the change impacts the whole organization or just a small department, the proper management of change is always important. A small-scale change could prove more difficult than one on a larger scale.

So, whether you're attempting to facilitate the workflow in your department, acquire new software, redesign a package, restructure your sales department, kick off a new ad campaign, revive employee commitment, or encourage innovation—your management skills will be tested.

All changes need to be managed. If you manage your change well, it will show. Your results will speak for themselves.

CHAPTER TWO WORKSHEET:
MANAGING YOUR CHANGE(S)

1. Change . . . whether you are contemplating it, planning it, or in the midst of it, what change are you currently facing in your organization?

_____

_____

_____

_____

_____

_____

_____

2. How can you personally benefit from successfully participating in the management of this change?

_____

_____

_____

_____

_____

_____

3. List specific reasons or organizational issues creating the need for this change.

_____

_____

_____

_____

_____

_____

_____

4. What can you do to begin helping your organization manage this change?

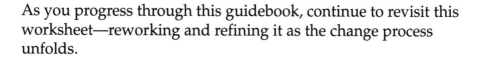

_____

_____

_____

_____

_____

_____

As you progress through this guidebook, continue to revisit this worksheet—reworking and refining it as the change process unfolds.

THE SIX-STEP CHANGE PROCESS

Change demands direct attention to detail, otherwise it causes tension, confusion, and ultimately, counterproductivity. You can't expect any organizational change to be successful unless you plan it proficiently, implement it strategically, and evaluate it fully.

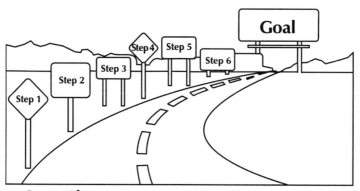

Start Change Management Process

This chapter outlines exactly how to attempt a successful change using a six-step process. Think of this six-step change process as your overall road map. If you put it into practice, it will help you facilitate successful change by steering you past unwelcome pitfalls and ensuring that you cover all grounds.

Following the steps in this process will involve you and your change team in six challenging, different phases. By taking the time to delve into each step, you'll see your vision of change crystallize. And you'll also receive greater acceptance from all of those involved.

So, get acquainted with the six-step change process!

A Model For Managed Change

Here's a brief explanation of each step in the change process.

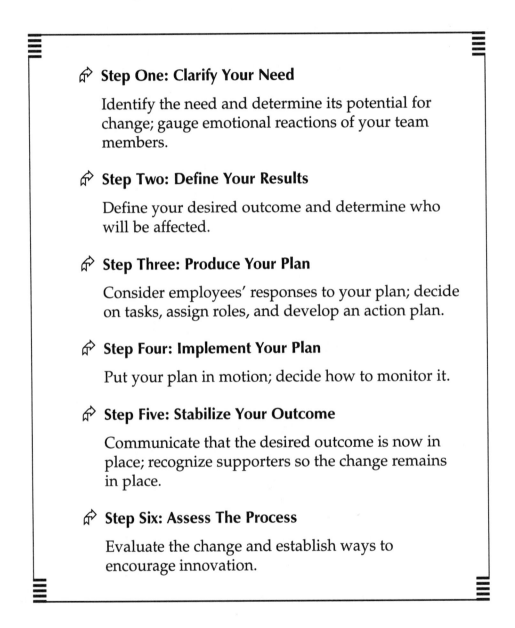

☞ **Step One: Clarify Your Need**

Identify the need and determine its potential for
change; gauge emotional reactions of your team
members.

☞ **Step Two: Define Your Results**

Define your desired outcome and determine who
will be affected.

☞ **Step Three: Produce Your Plan**

Consider employees' responses to your plan; decide
on tasks, assign roles, and develop an action plan.

☞ **Step Four: Implement Your Plan**

Put your plan in motion; decide how to monitor it.

☞ **Step Five: Stabilize Your Outcome**

Communicate that the desired outcome is now in
place; recognize supporters so the change remains
in place.

☞ **Step Six: Assess The Process**

Evaluate the change and establish ways to
encourage innovation.

Each step in this process is explained in greater detail in the
following chapters, which include an in-depth look at how one
organization used these steps to master a specific change scenario.

CHAPTER THREE WORKSHEET:
USING THE SIX-STEP CHANGE PROCESS

1. Where in the six-step change process is your team? Place an "X" along the continuum line to indicate the current position of the change process with which you're involved.

Step:　　1　　　2　　　3　　　4　　　5　　　6

2. What does the "X" tell you?

_____

_____

_____

For example, an "X" over Step # 4 indicates that you are already implementing a change, yet have you taken time to clarify need and communicate it to others *(Step 1)*? If not, some quick action is going to be required to minimize resistance.

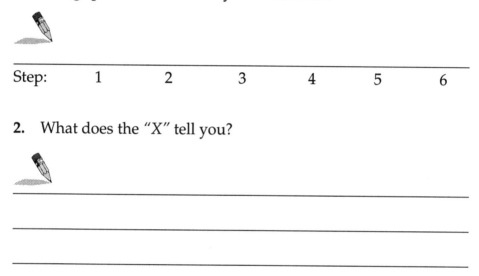

Or perhaps your "X" looks more like this:

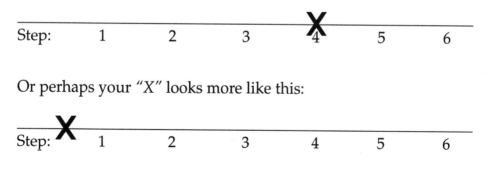

Are you just now contemplating change? If so, now's the time to delve into each step of the change management process!

STEP ONE: CLARIFY YOUR NEED

*"In prosperity, prepare for a change;
in adversity, hope for one."*

Anonymous

The first step in managing a successful change is to clarify the need for change—to discover all the answers you can to this question: *"Why change?"*

If your only answer to that question is, *"Because upper management said so,"* then you need to reexamine the issue. Search for valid reasons to change. If you still come up with the same answer, or you're reaching too hard for obscure reasons, then question those who advocate the change.

Why Change?

> ☞ What *"organizational cues"* indicate the need for change?
>
> ☞ What opportunities, benefits, or advantages exist?

If your proposed change is *"creative,"* you'll uncover *"organizational cues"* that indicate your need for change. Perhaps sales have been slipping, your computers are constantly down, or customers have been complaining. Such *"cues"* are flags that indicate change needs to take place.

If your proposed change is *"proactive,"* you'll need to decide what opportunities, benefits, or advantages will occur as a result of change. For example, will enacting the change help you gain a greater market share, increase employee satisfaction *(which leads to better employee retention)*, or perhaps appeal to a broader segment of the population? Explore all the possibilities.

Only when you are absolutely certain of the need for change should you continue with the change management process.

Let's see how employees of a specific company . . .

Delta, Inc., addressed their need for positive change management, beginning with a detailed account of how they followed Step One. . . .

Delta, Inc. was ready . . .

to tackle a change. The management team, noting a drop in their Customer Satisfaction Index, followed a problem-solving model to pinpoint the problem. They discovered that customer service personnel resolved only 80 percent of problems and issues reported by customers.

The customer service personnel weren't equipped to adequately answer technical problems. So when a customer called with a technical difficulty, the customer service representative would take a message and then forward it to the Technical Support Department. However, since responding to customer problems wasn't the top priority for the Technical Support Department, they often did not resolve the problems quickly enough for the customer, if they were resolved at all.

The management team decided that a change was in order. They wanted 100 percent of customer-related issues satisfactorily resolved. So they chose Mark, their Customer Service Manager, to spearhead a team responsible for the change.

The team's mandate: **Increase Customer Satisfaction!**

The change team's challenge: **Manage the change process so the goal becomes reality!**

Increase

Customer

Satisfaction!

Mark was very much aware . . .

of the problem in his department. After all, he was the one who initially brought the drop in the Customer Satisfaction Index to the attention of the management team. The morale of the Customer Service Department was slipping, and Mark could easily understand how change was essential to the success of his department. Thus, Mark was able to adequately justify the need for change.

Like Mark, once you resolve the issue of need in your own company, you're then responsible for choosing a group of reliable employees to assist you in spearheading the change process. Together, as the *"change team,"* you'll work toward the goal of a successful, productive change.

The Delta Change Management Team

Mark   Randy   Claire   Don   Ahmed

Mark chose the following individuals . . .

to serve as *"change agents"* on his team:

Mark - Customer Service Manager *(and team leader)*,

Randy - Technical support representative,

Claire - Customer service representative,

Don - Customer service representative, and

Ahmed - Marketing representative. . . .

After he chose his change agents . . .

Mark assembled his team for their first meeting. Claire and Don were two of his employees in Delta's Customer Service Department. They were selected for their large *"sphere of influence"* among the other employees in his department. Randy, the technical support representative, had been instrumental in the problem-solving process that the management team initiated, so he was already familiar with the solutions they would study. Finally, Mark felt that Ahmed, the marketing representative, would help them understand the scope of the problem, since Delta's expanding product line seemed to compound the problem. . . .

One issue you'll immediately have to resolve with your group is the *"acceptance factor."* Your team members need to be as certain of the need for change as you are.

"We need to change" . . .

Mark began, as he presented his supporting facts to the group.

Claire was immediately defensive. *"Why don't you look at the positive side?"* she argued. *"We're satisfying 80 percent of our customers. That's a big chunk."*

"Yeah," Don agreed. *"Besides, it's not our fault these figures are low. The Technical Support Department has been no support at all."* That irked Randy, and the two began a heated exchange.

Meanwhile, Mark sat back and jotted down his team's reactions on a notepad. He knew there would be resistance to the change, and he wanted to address their specific concerns. So, he recorded their reactions without saying a word. . . .

Because the reactions were mostly negative . . .

Mark decided that outlining the pros and cons on a Force Field Diagram, a tool used to identify obstacles to reaching a goal, would help broaden the team members' perspectives. So, Mark objectively listed the negative emotions *(restraining forces)* that were keeping his team from understanding and accepting the change, and then counteracted them by listing the facts *(driving forces)* that emphasized the need for change. Mark's Force Field Diagram looked like this:

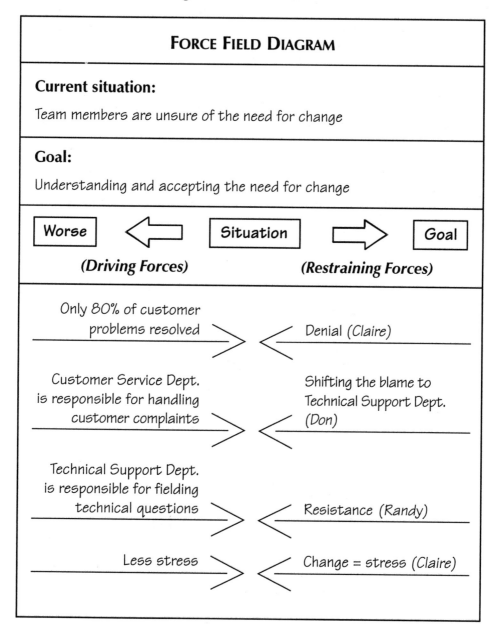

FORCE FIELD DIAGRAM

Current situation:

Team members are unsure of the need for change

Goal:

Understanding and accepting the need for change

| Worse | ⟸ | Situation | ⟹ | Goal |

(Driving Forces)   **(Restraining Forces)**

| Only 80% of customer problems resolved | Denial (Claire) |

| Customer Service Dept. is responsible for handling customer complaints | Shifting the blame to Technical Support Dept. (Don) |

| Technical Support Dept. is responsible for fielding technical questions | Resistance (Randy) |

| Less stress | Change = stress (Claire) |

The initial reactions of the change team . . .

were good indicators of how the other employees might react. By filling out the Force Field Diagram, Mark realized that, based on his change team's reactions, the responses from the Customer Service and Technical Support Departments would not be positive. This convinced Mark once again of the need for proper planning by the change team.

Mark praised Don and Claire for their ability to work in a stressful environment. *"It's frustrating to have to deal with customer complaints you can't resolve on your own,"* said Mark. They agreed. By responding to their concerns with facts, Mark finally convinced them that a change, though certainly not easy, would be to their benefit.

Randy was easier to persuade. Although he understood and accepted the need for change, he was caught off guard when Don blamed his department. Ahmed was all for the change; from a marketing standpoint, a satisfied customer is a repeat customer.

The Delta, Inc. team made a point of looking at possible hurdles to the change at an early stage. They considered the *"change acceptance factor,"* the extent to which those involved in the change were willing to accept, work on, and participate in the change process.

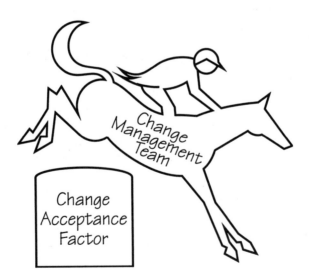

Don't fall into the trap of showing little or no concern about whether your employees understand the need for change. They care. And their support is vital to your success in managing change.

Also consider these other traps, which could sabotage the change process:

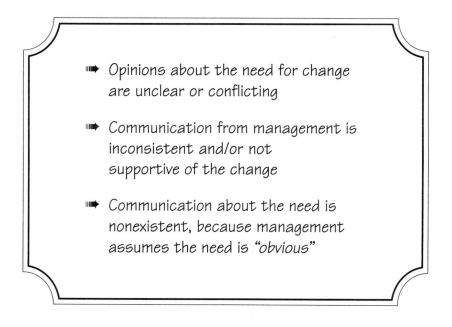

- ➠ Opinions about the need for change are unclear or conflicting

- ➠ Communication from management is inconsistent and/or not supportive of the change

- ➠ Communication about the need is nonexistent, because management assumes the need is "obvious"

If you can avoid these traps, you'll be ready to tackle Step Two in the change process.

CHAPTER FOUR WORKSHEET:
CLARIFYING YOUR NEED FOR CHANGE

1. What *"organizational cues"* are behind your change?

_____

_____

_____

2. List any opportunities, benefits, or advantages that will occur as a result of your change.

_____

_____

_____

3. Who will you select as members of your change team, and why?

Who	Why
_____	_____
_____	_____
_____	_____
_____	_____
_____	_____

4. Use the Force Field Diagram below to identify the forces that are driving and those that are restraining your team/ organization from reaching its goal.

Note: There is a blank Force Field Diagram form in the Appendix for you to reproduce and use.

FORCE FIELD DIAGRAM

Current situation:

Goal:

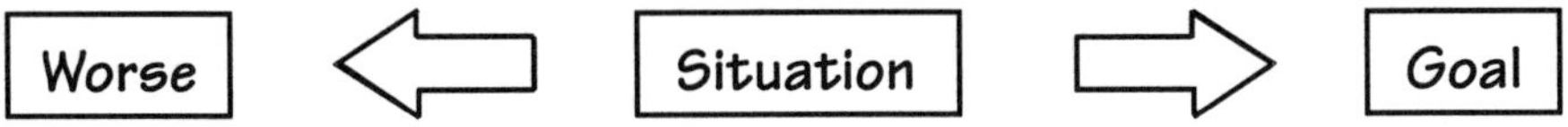

| Worse | ⇐ | Situation | ⇒ | Goal |

(Driving Forces)   *(Restraining Forces)*

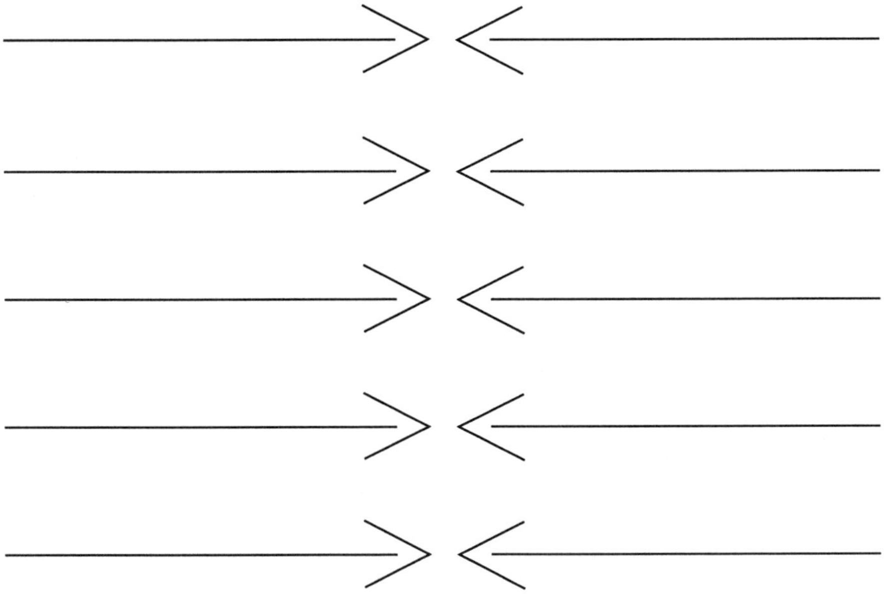

———————————————————→<———————————————————

———————————————————→<———————————————————

———————————————————→<———————————————————

———————————————————→<———————————————————

———————————————————→<———————————————————

STEP TWO: DEFINE YOUR RESULTS

> *"All human progress, like baseball, involves a certain amount of risk. You can't steal second while keeping one foot on first."*
>
> Anonymous

You know you need to change. You've convinced yourself and your change team that it's not only necessary, but advantageous. Now you're ready to settle on the specifics. Step Two, defining your results, consists of these goals:

- ☞ **Decide on your desired outcome**
- ☞ **Determine its feasibility**
- ☞ **Consider its evaluation**
- ☞ **Recognize who will be affected**

A change that takes place without a specific goal is mismanaged change—one that will never live up to expectations *(or even come close).* Clearly defining your result will point you in the right direction. If you follow the guidelines in this chapter, you'll have plenty of ammunition to prepare for a successful change.

Take a look at how you can successfully define your goals and watch how the Delta change team defined theirs.

Decide On Your Desired Outcome

What do you hope your change will do for your organization? Consumer products companies almost routinely repackage successful products as *"new and improved"* as a signal of a change for consumers. Their desired outcome is increased sales. For example, a large Japanese manufacturer relocated a number of American managers and their families to Japan for two or three years for consultation and brainstorming; they hoped that this would increase productivity in American plants.

These two examples reveal general, common goals: increase sales and productivity. It's essential to identify such *"greater"* goals. By keeping that goal at the forefront, you'll be able to plan and organize to meet the *"greater"* goals and subgoals *(or targets)* along the way.

Let's see how Delta managed this step . . .

Mark invited Misha, the Technical Support Manager, and Omar, one of Misha's employees, to the change team's second meeting. Misha had led a problem-solving group on this issue, so she was not only aware of the issue, but had proposed solutions to the customer service problem.

Mark began the meeting by saying, *"Our goal, according to the management team, is to increase customer satisfaction by resolving 100 percent of customer issues that are brought to our attention. Now that's a great goal,"* and here he paused, *"but we need to specify exactly how the Customer Service and Technical Support Departments will successfully handle that goal."*

Mark then deferred to Misha, who described the solutions her problem-solving team had devised:

Solutions

✔ Train customer service personnel to handle the most technical problems

✔ Establish a hot line between Customer Service and Technical Support Departments, so difficult problems can be handled more efficiently

"Those are great solutions,"...

Mark interceded, *"but we need to be more specific. For example, should we shoot for the Customer Service Department to handle 50 percent of the technical problems? Or 75 percent? Why don't we brainstorm to settle on the specifics."* Don agreed to record the ideas on a flip chart.

Mark called a halt to the brainstorming after a few minutes, and then the team pared down their ideas to this clearly focused outcome:

Increase customer satisfaction by resolving 100 percent of customer problems:

✔ 90 percent of customer technical questions will be handled by customer service personnel

✔ No more than 10 percent should need to be handled by technical support personnel

✔ Customer service personnel are responsible for resolving all customer problems within 24 hours

Determine Its Feasibility

Can it be done? Address the question of feasibility before it's too late. You don't want to discover after the fact that the costly and/or time-consuming change you implemented won't result in your desired outcome.

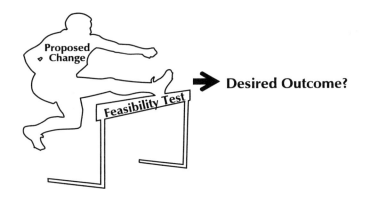

Omar, the technical support representative . . .

who came to the meeting with Misha, was skeptical of the hot line Delta wanted to set up between customer service and technical support. Misha's problem-solving team had decided it would be nearly as effective as training the customer service personnel, but Omar had his doubts. *"I don't see that it would help that much,"* he said. *"Most technical support reps, including myself, would probably take a message and tell the customers we'd get back to them. But then we'd sit on it. The only difference between this new way and the old system,"* he explained, *"would be that we, not the customer service reps, would write the message."*

Omar's point was well-taken. The change team then brainstormed some more and came up with the idea of a *"buddy system."* Each customer service rep would be paired-off with a technical support rep *(and a back-up in case of absenteeism or other problems)*. Responsibility would be the key difference. For example, if Claire and Randy were paired, they'd be responsible for each other. Claire would check to see if the problem was resolved within 24 hours. If a difficulty occurred, she would notify Misha.

In this instance, Delta maneuvered around the common pitfall of not allowing individuals with critical expertise or interests to provide suggestions. Omar saved the company some grief. The proposed change passed the feasibility test. . . .

Consider Its Evaluation

How will the desired outcome be evaluated? Without evaluation, who can prove that the goals were met or that the outcome was favorable?

> ### Delta already had a tracking system . . .
> in place. Each customer call was entered into their computer system, so the group only had to decide on how to monitor the buddy system. Claire agreed to create a workable form to track the time and success of each call. . . .

Recognize Who Will Be Affected

Recognizing everyone who will be affected by the change is a critical factor in the change management process. If you ignore those whom the change affects, watch out for problems further down the road. If you adequately consider everyone affected, your change will proceed much more smoothly.

> ### The Delta change team agreed . . .
> that the Customer Service and Technical Support Departments would be the primary departments affected. Ahmed, the marketing representative, thought his department could ease the change. *"No offense to technical support,"* he said, *"but I think having marketing help familiarize the customer service personnel with the new product line would be beneficial. We know some of the technical details, and I'll bet we can explain it in simpler terms."*

Before you proceed to Step Three, be aware of the following traps:

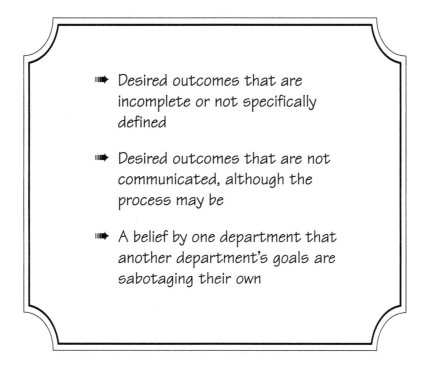

➠ Desired outcomes that are incomplete or not specifically defined

➠ Desired outcomes that are not communicated, although the process may be

➠ A belief by one department that another department's goals are sabotaging their own

CHAPTER FIVE WORKSHEET:
DEFINING YOUR RESULTS

1. What is your common *"greater"* goal?

_____

_____

_____

_____

_____

2. What will your change do for your team, department, work group, or organization? List your desired outcome*(s)*.

_____

_____

_____

_____

_____

3. How feasible is your result?

_____

_____

4. How will you evaluate your result?

_____

_____

_____

_____

_____

_____

_____

_____

_____

5. Who will your change affect?

_____

_____

_____

_____

_____

_____

_____

STEP THREE: PRODUCE YOUR PLAN

> *"There is no sadder or more frequent*
> *obituary on the pages of time than*
> *'We have always done it this way.'"*
>
> Anonymous

You're convinced of the need for change, and you've defined what you want your change to accomplish. Now it's time to put your plan together, one that will lead to your desired outcome. To do this, you'll need to:

☞ **Analyze the impacts and requirements**

☞ **Organize the plan**

Analyze The Impacts And Requirements

If you conscientiously analyze the impact of your change and the requirements to successfully implement it, you're well on your way to managing a successful change. Too many managers neglect this important step; they feel that analysis is a waste of time. But it's not. Analyzing the impacts and requirements is critical for productive change, so it's important to consider the following:

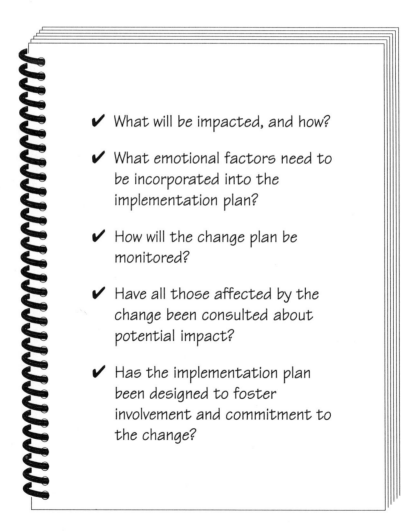

✔ What will be impacted, and how?

✔ What emotional factors need to be incorporated into the implementation plan?

✔ How will the change plan be monitored?

✔ Have all those affected by the change been consulted about potential impact?

✔ Has the implementation plan been designed to foster involvement and commitment to the change?

What will be impacted, and how?

Previously, your change team decided who will be affected by the change. Now it's time to decide what the specific impacts will be. Check to see if any of these areas will be affected:

⟹ Mission/values/culture/organizational structure

⟹ Human resources *(skills, etc.)*

⟹ Management practices; employee roles and responsibilities

⟹ Products and services

Once you've identified what your change will impact, determine how it will be impacted. Maybe you'll discover that you need to redesign your work group or organizational structure, clarify your mission, rewrite job descriptions, reorganize your management practices, and/or emphasize a certain product or service.

By taking care of these issues before you implement your change, you won't have to retrace steps. It'll save you time, money, and stress.

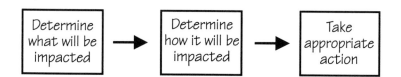

The Delta change team . . .

found a number of areas which would be impacted by the upcoming change. The team members discovered that they would have to rewrite job descriptions for both customer service and technical support representatives; both Mark and Misha would need to alter their management practices to incorporate the change; and customer satisfaction would become a top priority, which would definitely have an impact on the mission of the organization. . . .

What emotional factors need to be incorporated into the implementation plan?

Consider ways to manage:

➠ Resistance, anxiety, anger.

➠ Enthusiasm/excitement.

Emotions run high whenever a change is in progress. Whether your employees react positively or negatively, learning how to manage their emotions will ensure that your change doesn't veer from its course. You want to accomplish your desired result, and emotions can block your effort.

The challenge of dealing with emotions in the midst of change can be daunting.

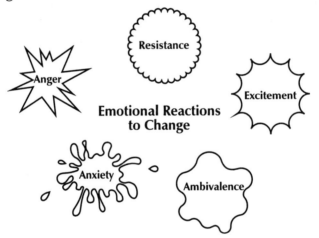

Mark was exposed to a variety of emotions . . .
when the members of his change team debated the need for change. He asked the team to identify the emotional reactions they and other members of the Customer Service and Technical Support Departments might experience over the next few weeks as they changed their processes for handling customer questions and problems. The response covered the spectrum from anger to ambivalence. Managing this aspect of the change was essential to their success. . . .

Note: This area is so important, an entire chapter is devoted to revealing how you can manage resistance to your change *(see Chapter Ten, Encouraging Commitment to Change).*

How will the change plan be monitored?

Considerations include:

⟶ Who will direct your change plan?

⟶ Who should be involved in identifying and resolving key issues?

⟶ What kind of tracking system will you use?

⟶ What methods will you use to incorporate additional points into your change plan?

These considerations will help ensure that your change will do what it's supposed to—lead you to your goal!

The Delta change team . . .

unanimously decided that Mark and Misha would direct the change plan. The team itself was responsible for identifying and resolving any key issues, which they had been doing all along. They had discussed the tracking system at the last meeting, and Claire handed out copies of the form she'd devised to track the time and success of each problem call. The Delta change team was already monitoring issues and potential problems. They would continue meeting throughout the change process to take care of all concerns. . . .

Have all those affected by the change been consulted about potential impact?

This is a recurring theme in the management of any change process. It may seem redundant to keep stressing your change's impact, but doing so will prove the difference between a change that goes awry and one that excels.

At Delta, Don conducted a survey . . .

among all customer service personnel. Results showed that the extra workload concerned some reps, while others questioned whether they could gain the technical expertise needed to solve 90 percent of their customers' technical concerns. Mark thanked Don for his help and decided to schedule a meeting with all of his customer service employees to address their concerns. In so doing, he considered the next question. . . .

Has the implementation plan been designed to foster involvement and commitment to the change?

Help your employees by keeping the *"greater"* goal foremost in their minds. Keep the goal and its means closely intertwined for a more easily managed change.

Also emphasize the benefits to your employees. Knowing a change will benefit them increases their involvement and commitment. Brainstorm ways to add incentives for your employees, and don't overlook psychological incentives. A thank-you note or a sentence of praise can go a long way toward making your employees feel that they are essential to your success.

In Delta's case . . .

Mark realized that reinforcing their goal to increase customer satisfaction was more effective than merely discussing the means to that goal, such as learning more technical details, working with technical support reps, etc. He kept focusing on this goal to encourage involvement, both of the team members, and of others at Delta who were affected by the change. . . .

Avoid these potential traps when analyzing the impacts and requirements of your change:

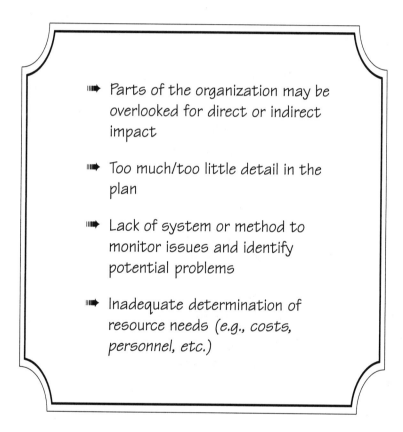

- ⟶ Parts of the organization may be overlooked for direct or indirect impact

- ⟶ Too much/too little detail in the plan

- ⟶ Lack of system or method to monitor issues and identify potential problems

- ⟶ Inadequate determination of resource needs (e.g., costs, personnel, etc.)

Organize Your Change Plan

Once you've completed the analysis of your plan's impacts and requirements, you're ready to write your change plan in detail. You've reached the point where you can describe the specifics of who will do what, and when.

When writing your change plan, consider these questions:

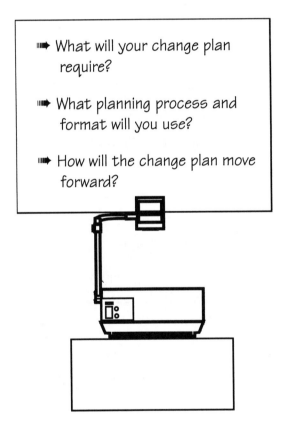

➡ What will your change plan require?

➡ What planning process and format will you use?

➡ How will the change plan move forward?

What will your change plan require?

➠ Time

➠ Money

➠ Acting managers

➠ Consultants

➠ New roles

If this seems to be a repeat of your impact analysis, don't despair. Your analysis laid the groundwork by helping you identify the plan's underlying requirements.

Change Plan Requirements

Delta realized that their change . . .

would require new job descriptions for customer service and technical support personnel. The change team listed the rewriting of job descriptions as an actual task, determined who would be responsible for it, and estimated how much it would cost to implement. . . .

What planning process and format will you use?

Formulate an overall plan of major activities and a detailed plan of specific responsibilities.

When Delta's change team arrived . . .

at the next meeting, Mark was eager. *"We've finally reached the point,"* he said, *"where we can list actual tasks and who's responsible for them."* He paused for a moment. *"The change is getting closer and closer. Are we ready to proceed?"*

Claire and Don moved forward in their chairs. They were involved in the groundwork up to this point and were eager to move ahead. At the Customer Service Department meeting, Mark had allowed them to field the question-and-answer session, and they were able to convince the other employees that the change would be beneficial. With Mark's approval, Claire hung banners on the department walls, proclaiming, *"We're ready for a change!"* and *"100 percent of customer problems solved is our goal!"* Meanwhile, Don surveyed the employees again, this time to determine their technical knowledge.

Mark had previously decided that filling out a Task/Responsibility Matrix would help the change team at this point in planning. *"A Task/Responsibility Matrix will help clarify our specific assignments and responsibilities,"* he explained. He drew the matrix on a flip chart and asked Ahmed to record the group's responses.

"First, we need to identify our tasks," Mark said. *"What tasks will our change involve?"* As the team chose the major tasks, Ahmed recorded them on the left side of the matrix. . . .

Next, the change team decided . . .

which team members and departments would be responsible for the tasks. For each task, a *"P"* was assigned to represent a primary responsibility, an *"S"* if it was a secondary responsibility, a *"C"* if the person or group needed to be in the communication loop, a *"+"* if the rating demanded extra emphasis, and it was left blank if there was no relationship between an individual or a department and the task.

Here's a look at one portion of the change team's Task/Responsibility Matrix:

TASK/RESPONSIBILITY MATRIX

TASK	RESPONSIBILITY							
	Mark	Misha	Randy	Don	Claire	Ahmed	Omar	Personnel
Survey customer service personnel to determine skill level and gaps	C			P	S			
Survey technical support personnel to discover most frequently asked technical questions	C	S	P					
Design training program	C	S+	S					P
Conduct training	C	S+	S			S		P
Acquire and install hot line, software, and hardware	C	P						

P = Primary responsibility   S = Secondary responsibility   C = Communication loop

Mark asked the team members . . .

to return to the next meeting with a more detailed plan and an idea of the
cost for each task they were responsible for. . . .

Include project timetables in your plan, and consider contingency
plans, feedback, and communication systems.

Delta's change team . . .

was prepared at its next session. Mark got them immediately involved in
filling out an action plan for the change. Their action plan was an extension
of their Task/Responsibility Matrix. Along with the task and responsible
person and/or group, it included the projected dates, an estimation of the
hours involved, and the cost.

Here is a portion of the change team's action plan:

ACTION PLAN					
ACTION STEP/ TASK	**RESPONSIBLE PERSON/TEAM**	**BEGIN DATE**	**END DATE**	**EST. HOURS**	**EST. COST**
Survey technical support personnel to discover most frequently asked technical questions	Randy and Misha	1/10	1/24	20	$600
Design training program	Misha, Randy, and Personnel	1/29	2/7	200	$6000
Conduct training	Misha, Randy, Ahmed, and Personnel	2/12	3/35	20-40	$600 -$1200

Don't forget to consider contingency plans for the different tasks in your action plan. That way you can cover your bases if some kink occurs in your operation or you're too pressed for time to finish your task.

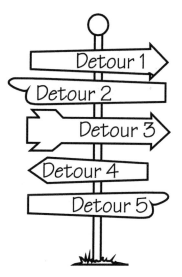

In Delta's case . . .

the team decided that if personnel didn't have the expertise or time to help design the training program, they would hire consultants. So Mark asked Misha to work with personnel in locating reputable consultants who could help them.

The Delta change team also decided that informal surveys of both customer service and technical support personnel would provide the change team with feedback on the change process. Instead of giving the managers this task, the team decided that the employees would be more open with colleagues. So Claire and Don volunteered to keep open the communication channel between management and the Customer Service Department, while Randy volunteered himself and said he'd ask Omar to help in obtaining feedback from the Technical Support Department.

How will the change plan move forward?

When you intend to implement any change in an organization, you can't pretend it won't affect people. Yes, you've already convinced your employees of the need. Yes, you've consulted them about the impact of your change. But if you leave them out of the game now, you'll have an uproar on your hands.

Factor in how you'll kick off the change, get progress updates, and keep your employees charged up. If these concerns are part of your action plan, managing your change will be easier.

Watch out for these common pitfalls:

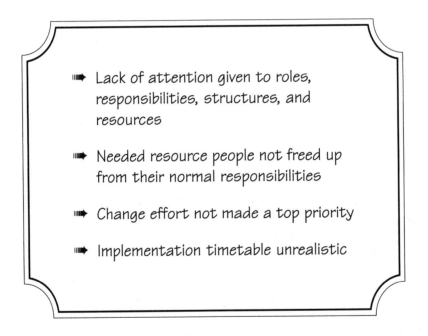

> ➠ Lack of attention given to roles, responsibilities, structures, and resources
>
> ➠ Needed resource people not freed up from their normal responsibilities
>
> ➠ Change effort not made a top priority
>
> ➠ Implementation timetable unrealistic

CHAPTER SIX WORKSHEET:
PRODUCING YOUR PLAN

A. Analyzing Impacts and Requirements

1. List all areas that will be impacted by your change, and explain how.

   WHAT   HOW

_____

_____

_____

_____

_____

_____

2. Identify the emotions you expect from employees during implementation of the change:

_____

_____

_____

_____

_____

3. Describe your process to monitor the change plan.

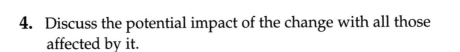

_____

_____

_____

_____

4. Discuss the potential impact of the change with all those affected by it.

_____

_____

_____

_____

5. How will you gain involvement and commitment to your change?

_____

_____

_____

_____

_____

_____

B. Organizing Your Change Plan

1. Complete a detailed Task/Responsibility Matrix for the upcoming change in your organization. Be sure to include all the tasks that need to be done, and the team members or departments responsible for them. For each task, assign a rating for each team member or department: a *"P"* indicates a primary responsibility, an *"S"* a secondary responsibility, a *"C"* if the person or group needs to be in the communication loop, a *"+"* if the rating demands extra emphasis, and a blank if there is no relationship between an individual or a department and the task.

Note: There is a blank matrix form in the Appendix for you to reproduce and use.

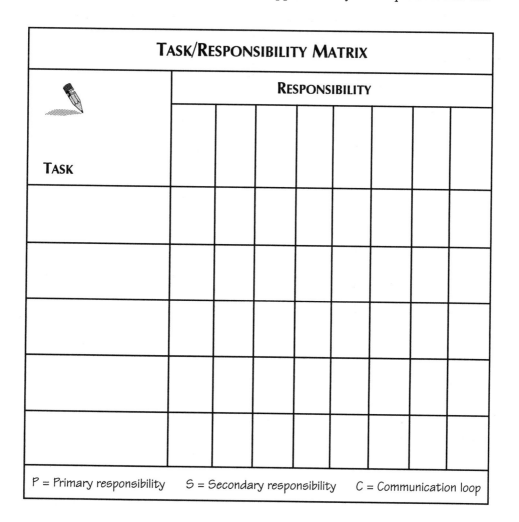

TASK/RESPONSIBILITY MATRIX

RESPONSIBILITY

TASK

P = Primary responsibility   S = Secondary responsibility   C = Communication loop

2. Complete a detailed action plan for the upcoming change in your organization. Be sure to include tasks, person(s) responsible, timetables, estimated hours, and estimated cost. Once you are finished with your action plan, compare it to your Task/Responsibility Matrix.

Note: There is a blank action plan form in the Appendix for you to reproduce and use.

ACTION PLAN					
ACTION STEP/ TASK	RESPONSIBLE PERSON/TEAM	BEGIN DATE	END DATE	EST. HOURS	EST. COST

3. How will you:

a) Kick off your change?

b) Get progress updates?

c) Keep your employees involved and motivated?

STEP FOUR: IMPLEMENT YOUR PLAN

"One must never lose time in vainly regretting the past or in complaining against the changes which cause us discomfort, for change is the essence of life."

Anatole France

You've finally reached the point where you can put your plan into action. But it's not time to sit back and watch it progress unattended. To successfully implement your plan, take these points into consideration:

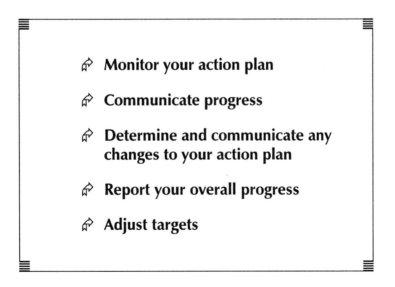

- ☞ **Monitor your action plan**

- ☞ **Communicate progress**

- ☞ **Determine and communicate any changes to your action plan**

- ☞ **Report your overall progress**

- ☞ **Adjust targets**

Monitor Your Action Plan

How will you monitor your action plan? This consideration is crucial, for you must keep a careful watch on the status of your change. Whether your change is being implemented over two weeks or two years, if you aren't monitoring it, there's a greater chance it'll veer off its course and not reach the desired destination.

> ### *Even though Delta's action plan . . .*
> would take two and one-half months to implement, the change team decided to meet twice a week to monitor progress. Mark *(along with Don and Claire)* and Misha *(with the help of Randy and Omar)* kept daily tabs on the employees in their departments. The twice-weekly meetings covered issues *"by exception only"* to save time. They only reported problems, difficulties, and unresolved issues. . . .

Communicate Progress

Another important consideration deals with the handling of progress communication. How will you manage this? Remember that the more you involve your employees in the change, the better. Don't ignore their input or disregard their views on how the change is progressing.

Input
Input
Input
Input
Input
_____
_____
_____
_____

The Delta change team . . .

felt that incorporating other people into small group sessions would provide them with feedback on how the employees were dealing with the change. So Claire, Don, Randy, and Omar began meeting with groups of four to five individuals for 45-minute feedback sessions. These small groups would not only provide feedback, but also identify other tasks that needed completion.

It was during one such feedback session that Randy realized he hadn't adequately prepared the technical support representatives for the change. When Delta began installing the hot line, the technical support reps rebelled. Randy hadn't surveyed the other employees or led small groups before the implementation, because he thought his fellow workers understood the change. But the technical support reps weren't aware that they were to be, in essence, responsible for answering all difficult technical questions within 24 hours.

This response from the technical support reps could have been avoided with proper planning. The Delta change team had fallen into a common trap. They neglected to double-check whether the Technical Support Department had really understood the need for change and had accepted the particular changes that were coming their way.

The Delta change team backtracked. Misha, along with Randy and Omar, held a departmental meeting and addressed the problem. They also arranged for each technical support rep to meet with his/her *"buddy"* in the Customer Service Department. Although this took extra time, the change team felt confident of both departments' commitments to the change. . . .

Determine And Communicate Any Changes To Your Action Plan

While monitoring your action plan, did you uncover any tasks that needed changing? Perhaps your progress communication indicated that certain tasks weren't going as well as planned. If you did your homework in Step 3 *(Produce Your Plan)*, then you'll have contingency plans already in place.

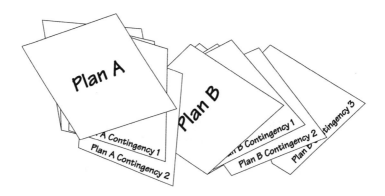

The Delta change team discovered . . .

that installing the new hot line system took much longer than anticipated. Because Misha needed to spearhead this task, she couldn't conduct the training of customer service personnel. The change team had to switch to its contingency plan. Omar led the training sessions, and a temporary replacement took over Omar's workload. . . .

Report Your Overall Progress

Your organization's administration may prefer that you manage the change and deal with the details, but when it comes to the results, they will be extremely interested in being part of the picture. To satisfy upper management's desire that you're handling the change successfully, report your overall progress. Don't assume, however, that the timing of those reports should be according to events within the change plan. Find out first when management wants to get progress reports and follow up accordingly. Treat them as your *(information)* customer!

The Delta change team's twice-weekly meetings . . .
and the department's small group sessions allowed Mark and Misha to keep close tabs on the change. After they successfully completed each task on the action plan, Mark reported the results to upper management. . . .

Adjust Targets

Will you be able to reach your goal? How will you know when you've achieved your desired outcome? The answers will be in your action plan. That is why you need to continually check whether your goal is in sight, if you will reach it, and when you have accomplished your end result.

Customer Service

Inquiry Response:

....

....

Monitoring and tracking indicated . . .

that Delta was headed in the right direction. Customer service personnel were confident they could handle a number of the technical questions, and the hot line actually worked. All callers received satisfactory answers within 24 hours. But the tracking system also revealed that the original goal of having customer service reps answer 90 percent of the technical questions was not achievable at that time. So the Delta change team adjusted their target; the reps would work toward answering 85 percent of the technical questions during this interim period. The adjustment allowed for the extra time it would take for customer service reps to gain technical expertise.

Don't get caught in these potential traps:

➠ Lack of effective tracking systems

➠ No contingency plans for unanticipated changes

➠ Implementation time frame too long; lack of continuity

➠ Change team members lose interest or no longer want to be involved

CHAPTER SEVEN WORKSHEET: IMPLEMENTING YOUR PLAN

1. How will you monitor your action plan?

_____

_____

_____

_____

2. How will you communicate progress to and from those affected?

_____

_____

_____

_____

3. How will you determine and communicate changes to your action plan?

_____

_____

_____

_____

4. How will you report overall progress to management?

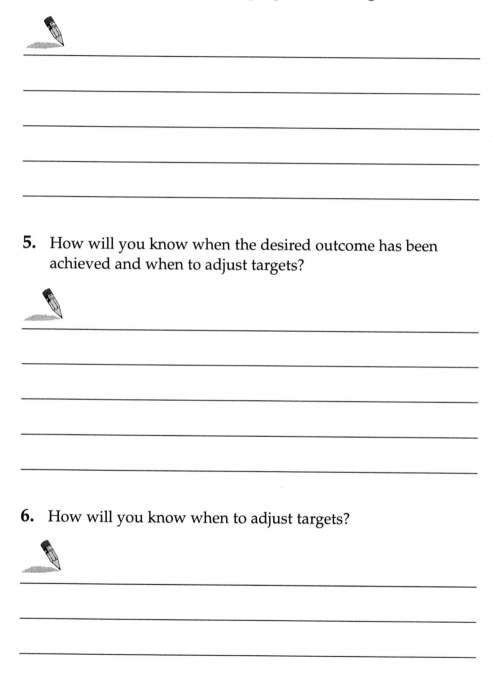

_____

_____

_____

_____

_____

5. How will you know when the desired outcome has been
achieved and when to adjust targets?

_____

_____

_____

_____

_____

6. How will you know when to adjust targets?

_____

_____

_____

_____

_____

STEP FIVE: STABILIZE YOUR OUTCOME

> *"Change does not necessarily assure progress, but progress implacably requires change . . . Education is essential to change, for education creates both new wants and the ability to satisfy them."*
>
> Henry Steele Commager

You've reached your goal. Have you finished managing your change? Not quite. You've hurdled the greatest obstacles, but you still have two steps remaining. This chapter discusses Step Five; what to do after you've implemented your change and you're satisfied with your result. *(Retrace your steps if you don't fall in this category.)*

You have undone the *"old way"* of doing things and succeeded in implementing a *"new way."* Now the challenge is to ensure this desired outcome, or *"new way"* becomes the standard. You'll need to stabilize the desired outcome, which requires that you:

☞ **Communicate that the desired outcome is now in place**

☞ **Provide recognition for those who supported the change**

Communicate That The Desired Outcome Is Now In Place

You've invested time, the organization's money, and your managing skills in the change process. You've implemented your change and reached your goal. Don't stop now! Employees can revert to their old ways, lose sight of the goal, and/or *"conveniently"* forget that a change ever took place. How do you call a halt to the change-reversal process or, better yet, keep it from kicking in? For starters, you need to always keep the *"greater"* goal in sight.

In Delta's case . . .

that meant reinforcing *"100 percent of customer problems resolved"* at every turn. Then you need to communicate that the desired outcome is in place. Unless it's *"frozen"* in its new position, the desired outcome can revert to its *"undesirable"* beginning. . . .

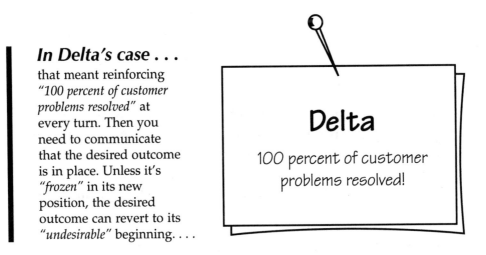

How do you do this? Perhaps you'll communicate a departmental change to your entire organization, or maybe you'll enlighten the public about an improvement through advertising.

The Delta change team . . .

had indeed reached their target of resolving 100 percent of customer problems, and their Customer Satisfaction Index was rising as a result. They decided to publicize the improvement in the Customer Satisfaction Index, but not to say specifically that they were resolving 100 percent of customer problems, preferring to say instead that they welcomed customer questions. They also froze the change by formalizing the new procedures and goals in their procedure manual, as well as by rewriting the job descriptions for both customer service and technical support personnel. And Delta trained new employees to reach the goals they set. . . .

Provide Recognition For Those Who Supported The Change

Give recognition to the employees who deserve it. This recognition is separate from the incentives you provided during the implementation of your change. Those incentives enabled you to move ahead faster; this recognition will ensure that your change doesn't move backward. And the employees who weren't as supportive will be watching closely. Recognize your *"change supporters,"* and your next change will be easier to manage.

At Delta, Mark began . . .

the first meeting after the change had been implemented with a solo standing ovation for his change team. *"Without you,"* he said, *"there would be no celebration. I could not have managed this change on my own. Your annual reviews,"* he added, *"will reflect your outstanding performance."*

The team then went to work devising ways to recognize their fellow employees who supported the change. They decided that all customer service reps who were handling 85-90 percent of technical calls on their own should be recognized in the company newsletter. Randy also suggested recognizing all effective *"buddy system"* pairs in the newsletter, and the change team agreed. The team also felt that customer testimonials on video would encourage all reps by letting them see firsthand how the customers appreciated the change.

Beware these potential traps when attempting to stabilize your
desired outcome:

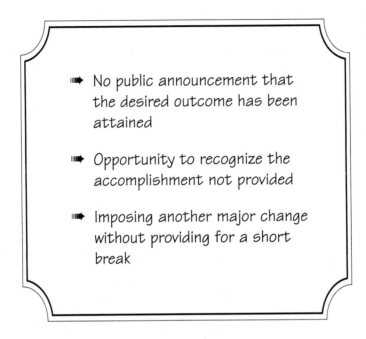

➠ No public announcement that
the desired outcome has been
attained

➠ Opportunity to recognize the
accomplishment not provided

➠ Imposing another major change
without providing for a short
break

CHAPTER EIGHT WORKSHEET: STABILIZING YOUR OUTCOME

1. List the different ways you will communicate that your desired outcome is now in place.

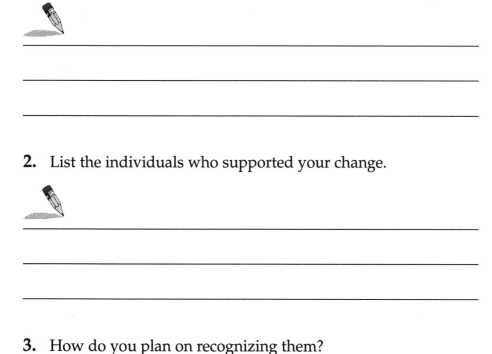

_____

_____

_____

2. List the individuals who supported your change.

_____

_____

_____

3. How do you plan on recognizing them?

_____

_____

_____

4. If you're considering another change in your organization, have you provided for a short break?

_____

STEP SIX: ASSESS THE PROCESS

"Progress comes from the intelligent use of experience."

Anonymous

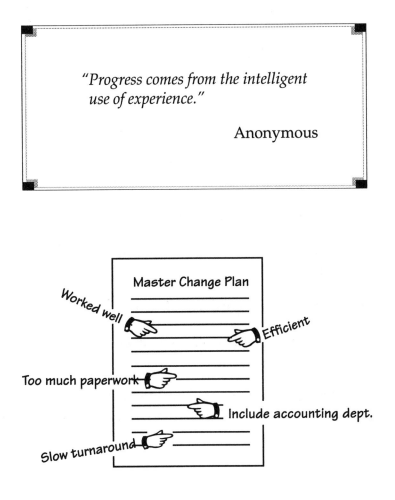

You've implemented your change and stabilized your desired outcome. You're nearing the end. Only one step remains in your effort to successfully manage change—assessing the process. You need to evaluate your complete change management process. Identify which steps were the smoothest and which ones you found to be the most difficult, and you'll be more than one step ahead the next time you tackle change.

Issues To Consider

To benefit from assessing the process, you must carefully consider the following questions:

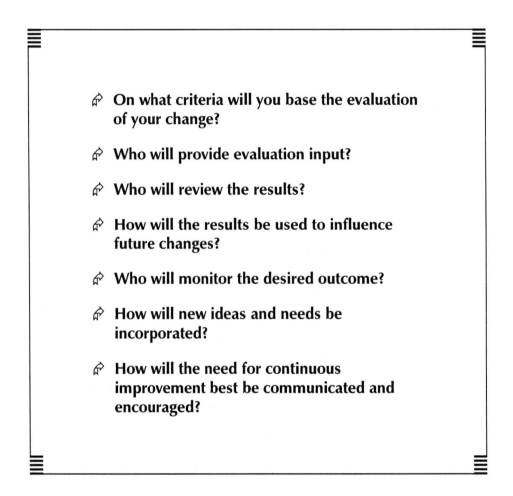

   ☞ **On what criteria will you base the evaluation of your change?**

   ☞ **Who will provide evaluation input?**

   ☞ **Who will review the results?**

   ☞ **How will the results be used to influence future changes?**

   ☞ **Who will monitor the desired outcome?**

   ☞ **How will new ideas and needs be incorporated?**

   ☞ **How will the need for continuous improvement best be communicated and encouraged?**

On what criteria will you base the evaluation of your change?

Think about:

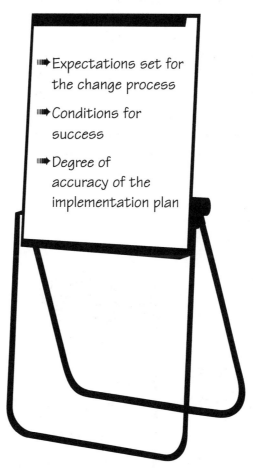

➠ Expectations set for the change process

➠ Conditions for success

➠ Degree of accuracy of the implementation plan

Expectations set for the change process

For example, did you think your change would increase sales 500 percent, and they only doubled? Or maybe you expected a change in workflow to increase productivity by 10 percent, and instead it rose by 50 percent. In the first case, you'd evaluate the change as a failure; in the second, an unprecedented success. But your evaluation should be in tune with realistic expectations.

> ### *The Delta change team readjusted . . .*
> the percentage of technical calls the customer service representatives should be able to handle *(from 90 percent to 85 percent)*, because the team realized it had set its expectations too high, a lesson learned for the next time. . . .

Conditions for success

You could also base your evaluation on whether you met certain conditions for success. For example, if you reached your desired outcome, but you spent a great deal more money than you had anticipated or ten of your employees quit during the process, your evaluation might not be as glowing as you expected. On the other hand, if you had to deal with phenomenal resistance or abnormal absenteeism, then you should consider those obstacles in your evaluation. Reaching your goal against such odds would result in high marks for you and your change team.

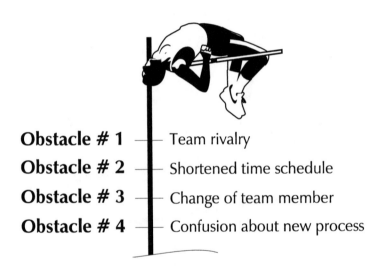

Obstacle # 1 — Team rivalry

Obstacle # 2 — Shortened time schedule

Obstacle # 3 — Change of team member

Obstacle # 4 — Confusion about new process

Degree of accuracy of the implementation plan

If you underestimated the time necessary to implement your change, your evaluation may appear less than wonderful. But if your desired outcome was realistic, and you accomplished your result, consider your change successful. It depends on how valid and accurate your targets are, and on the criteria you use to evaluate success.

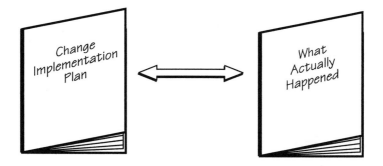

Who will provide evaluation input?

Definitely allow all those who were impacted by the change a chance to evaluate it. Their comments will prove invaluable. And don't think only in terms of employees.

The Delta change team . . .

not only distributed a questionnaire to customer service and technical support personnel, but Mark also interviewed customers who had called with questions, both before and after the change. Since the goal was improved customer satisfaction and resolution of 100 percent of customer problems, the input from these customers was a good indication of the success of the change. And, of course, the change team itself evaluated the process in depth. . . .

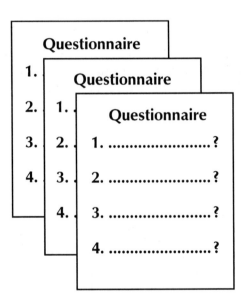

Who will review the results?

Will the results of the evaluation stay in the department if the change was strictly departmental or will upper management be privy to the information?

In Delta's case . . .

upper management expressed interest in seeing the results, since they had given Mark the mandate of improving customer satisfaction. Since they were pleased with the results, they asked Mark to share the change management process with other managers. . . .

How will the results be used to influence future changes?

Mistakes made or steps neglected in your change management process can be applied to future changes.

The Delta change team learned . . .

a lesson by overlooking the impact of the change on technical support reps. In future changes, that step *(considering the potential impact on all those affected)* would gain additional emphasis. . . .

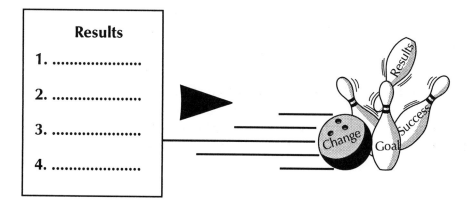

Who will monitor the desired outcome?

Ahmed said good-bye . . .

to the other members of the change team at the evaluation meeting. His role in the process had ended. The remaining four members—Mark, Claire, Don, and Randy—would continue to meet on a monthly basis to monitor the desired outcome and decide if further adjustments were necessary. . . .

How will new ideas and needs be incorporated?

Change is not static. Once you've stabilized your desired outcome, it may require adjustments or even a further change sometime in the future.

The Delta change team devised . . .

a way to stay abreast of the needs and ideas of customer service and technical support personnel. Twice a quarter the team planned to set up interviews with three to four reps from both departments.

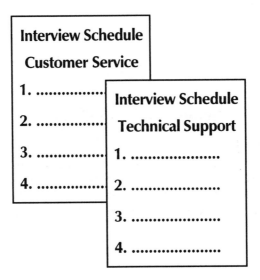

How will the need for continuous improvement best be communicated and encouraged?

Consider:

➡ Establishing systems for managers and associates to suggest improvements

➡ Identifying responsibilities for gathering suggestions

➡ Providing rewards for improvement suggestions

Organizations that encourage and reward innovation and participation find a higher degree of commitment and involvement among their employees.

Think about what it would mean to your organization if all employees were committed to the cause of improvement!

To learn from your change and to continue improving, don't fall into these potential traps:

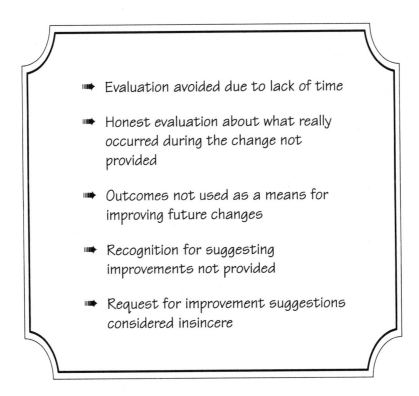

➡ Evaluation avoided due to lack of time

➡ Honest evaluation about what really occurred during the change not provided

➡ Outcomes not used as a means for improving future changes

➡ Recognition for suggesting improvements not provided

➡ Request for improvement suggestions considered insincere

CHAPTER NINE WORKSHEET:
ASSESSING YOUR PROCESS

1. How realistic were the expectations set for your change?

_____

_____

_____

2. Describe your conditions for success. Would they be different if you had to go through the process again?

_____

_____

_____

_____

_____

3. On what criteria will you base your evaluation?

_____

_____

_____

_____

4. Who in the organization have you identified as providers of evaluation input?

_____

_____

_____

5. Who will review your results?

_____

_____

6. Will you use your results to influence the planning of future changes? If so, how?

_____

_____

_____

_____

7. Who have you chosen to monitor your desired outcome?

_____

_____

8. How do you plan on incorporating new ideas and needs?

_____

_____

_____

_____

_____

_____

9. List the ways you will communicate and encourage the need for continuous improvement.

_____

_____

_____

_____

_____

_____

_____

_____

_____

ENCOURAGING COMMITMENT TO CHANGE

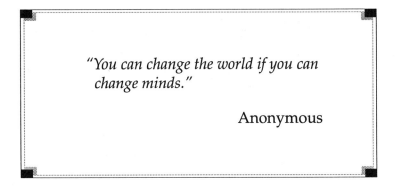

"You can change the world if you can change minds."

Anonymous

Successfully managing a change requires employee commitment at every step in the process. Whether you're in the planning, implementation, or even evaluation stage of change, you must always consider this human aspect. The *"people"* aspects are in a large part responsible for the success of a change. Part and parcel of managing a change is managing the people your change impacts.

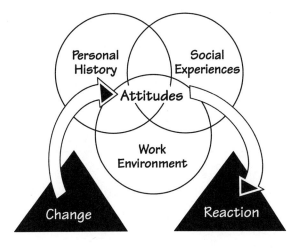

Attitudes About Change

It's not the change itself your employees resist—it's their attitudes about the change that determine whether or not they'll resist it.

Change will affect your employees in different ways, based on their attitudes and perceptions about change. It's important to realize that attitudes are both cognitive and highly emotional—our minds form the attitudes, and we often react to them on a gut level. Some employees' perceptions may be derived from common misconceptions about change, including the following:

MISCONCEPTION	REALITY
Misconception # 1: Change is the result of some negative occurrence.	Change can often be the result of regular and positive happenings (e.g., buying a new house, getting a promotion, a desire to improve, etc.).
Misconception # 2: Change means learning new behaviors or skills.	Change may only mean utilizing existing behaviors or skills in a different way.
Misconception # 3: Change is a stressful experience.	This is one of the more popular and common beliefs about change. If you perceive change as stressful, then it is! The implication in the misconception is that stress is always bad. Most people need some degree of change on a regular basis, and can benefit from new challenges.

Another reality is that people have a natural tendency to resist change. Anticipating, managing, and overcoming this resistance is the key to successful change.

Steps To Overcoming Resistance

You won't be able to avoid some degree of resistance to your change. But understanding the reasons behind it and working toward a goal of commitment to your change will point you toward productive change management. The following five steps illustrate how you can get the buy-in for your change. These steps supplement the overall six-step change process.

Use them when you need to *"exit"* from the systematic approach in the six-step model for managed change to focus instead on the human element of resistance to change.

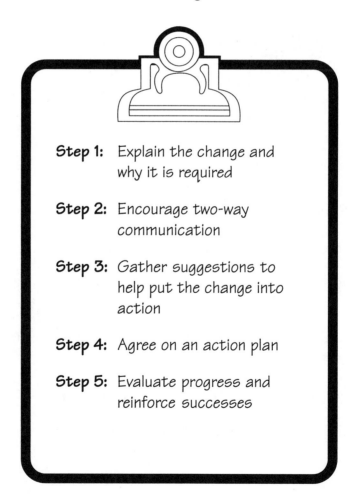

Step 1: Explain the change and why it is required

Step 2: Encourage two-way communication

Step 3: Gather suggestions to help put the change into action

Step 4: Agree on an action plan

Step 5: Evaluate progress and reinforce successes

Step 1: Explain the change and why it is required

➡ Clarify the need for change. People are more receptive to change when they understand why it's necessary.

➡ Help people understand how they are affected, and in what ways they can benefit from change.

Two-way communication

Step 2: Encourage two-way communication

➡ Get reactions and resistance out in the open.

➡ Clarify misunderstandings and respond to objections.

Step 3: Gather suggestions to help put the change into action

➡ Help eliminate personal fears of the unknown.

➡ Build a sense of control and involvement in the change.

Step 4: Agree on an action plan

➠ Collaborate with the change agents and sponsors; identify who does what and when.

➠ Establish commitments and accountabilities.

➠ Focus on opportunities and desired outcomes.

➠ Provide resources to implement the change plan.

Step 5: Evaluate progress and reinforce successes

➠ Ensure that plans are progressing. Make adjustments as needed.

➠ Provide recognition for support and efforts.

➠ Reinforce progress by publicizing successes.

The change you must manage is not yours alone. It also belongs to the individuals who are affected. Stop the resistance before it threatens to undermine your change effort. Help your employees see the change as necessary and advantageous. Encourage them to participate, and reward them for their support. Their commitment to the change is essential.

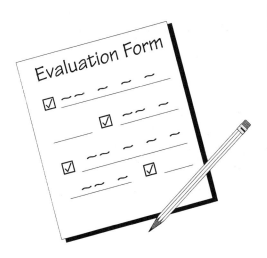

Attitudes Influence Behaviors

Your employees can respond to change in a variety of ways, including the following:

➠ Absenteeism

➠ Demotivation

➠ Verbal complaints and/or questions

➠ Motivation and increased effort

➠ Transfer requests

➠ Coming to work earlier

➠ Asking for more responsibility

➠ Resignations

If your employees respond negatively to a change, you'll be able to improve their perceptions if you can identify why they resist the change. Take a look at the following five *"personalities"* you may observe in individual resistance to change, and the strategies that will help you turn potential obstacles into opportunities.

Obstacles To Opportunities

Reason # 1: Scrooge-itis

Characteristics

➠ Primary focus is on economic factors.

➠ People hear through their wallets . . .
not through their ears.

Strategies

➠ Provide direct incentives.

➠ Ensure financial security.

➠ Increase earning potential.

➠ Provide cost/benefit analysis.

Reason # 2: Buried treasures

Characteristics

➡ Purpose and benefits of the change are not spelled out for those affected.

➡ Those affected are not involved in the planning and/or implementation.

Strategies

➡ Clarify specific and personal benefits.

➡ Involve those affected in the planning, implementation, and evaluation of the change.

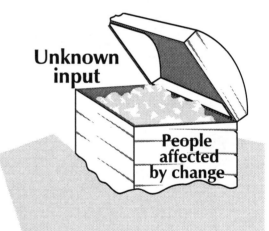

Unknown input

People affected by change

Reason # 3: Ugly baby syndrome

Characteristics

➡ People work hard to develop *"their"* way of doing something . . . they become parental.

➡ They may feel others are criticizing *"their baby."*

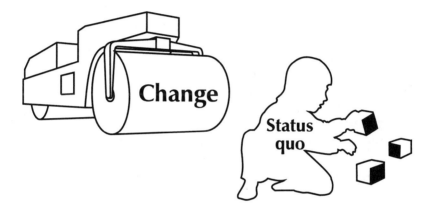

Strategies

➡ Avoid negative comments.

➡ Recognize the past and present ways as a foundation to build on.

➡ Focus on enhancements.

➡ Get direct involvement.

Reason # 4: Defensive fence building

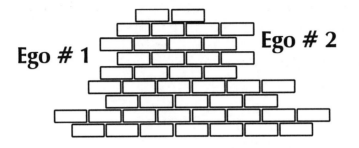

Ego # 1   Ego # 2

Characteristics

➡ People tend to put a fence around their egos by taking the change personally.

➡ Feelings of incompetence are stirred-up.

Strategies

➡ Stroke the egos.

➡ Demonstrate how direct involvement is necessary and advantageous to them.

➡ Ask for their help/advice.

Reason # 5: Comfortable habits

Characteristics

➠ People feel safe, secure, and comfortable in what they do.

➠ They take on the attitude of *"let's not upset the applecart"* and *"if it's not broke, then why fix it?"*

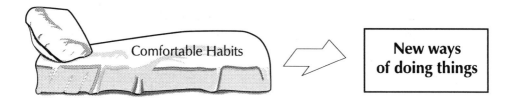

Comfortable Habits → New ways of doing things

Strategies

➠ Find good in the past and present ways.

➠ Focus on enhancements.

➠ Provide a taste-test to loosen attitudes and evaluate impacts in the near future.

➠ Relate the change to broad organizational goals.

CHAPTER TEN WORKSHEET:
CHALLENGES

How are you managing the human side of your change? Use this checklist to gauge your success in encouraging commitment to your change.

❑   1.   Change *(positive or negative)* is a potential threat to any individual, and therefore will almost always generate some degree of resistance.

❑   2.   Remember that associates will be more likely to change if they can help plan it. If possible, allow everyone affected by the change to contribute in some way to the implementation process. As a minimum, gather feedback from all those affected by the change.

❑   3.   Those affected by the change should have as much understanding of the change and its consequences as possible.

❑   4.   Place yourself in the shoes of those affected when planning a change.

❑   5.   Explain in simple and specific terms how people will benefit from the change.

❑   6.   Always maintain the self-esteem of those affected by the change.

❑　7.　Avoid creating win-lose situations whenever possible.

❑　8.　Determine the realistic level of commitment you need from those affected to successfully implement your change.

❑　9.　Collaborate with formal and informal leaders to gain their support.

❑　10.　Don't allow killer objections to grow into major obstacles. Look for ways to change negative concerns into positive opportunities.

❑　11.　Generate as few surprises as possible.

❑　12.　Remember that change of any kind demands a lot of unlearning as well as learning.

❑　13.　Be willing to lead by example on the job; demonstrate your behavioral support and commitment.

❑　14.　Develop concrete rewards and/or recognition for those who support the change.

❑　15.　Be willing to admit mistakes and learn from failures.

CHAPTER ELEVEN

SUMMARY

> *"Much of learning comes from experience in doing things, from working with people, from grappling with problems, from the exercise of judgment, and from mistakes."*
>
> Anonymous

Times have changed. It's no longer advantageous for an organization to stall when it comes to coping with the competition. It's no longer favorable to say, *"We've always done it this way."* Hesitate, and you're ejected from the conductor's seat. You must change to keep up with the times.

Yes, change has railroaded its way over many organizations in history. But if you plan your change well and invest your resources carefully, your fellow passengers will be amenable and you'll reach the right destination. Manage your change poorly, and you'll ride circles around the same track alone.

Be a dynamic leader. Get involved in the productive six-step change process and face all resistance head-on. Look at change as an adventure and persuade your employees to join you for the ride. Manage your change to travel a direct route to success.

REPRODUCIBLE FORMS

The following forms are provided for you to photocopy and use appropriately.

Force Field Diagram 106

Task/Responsibility Matrix 107

Action Plan 108

Force Field Diagram

Current situation:

Goal:

| Worse | ⇐ | Situation | ⇒ | Goal |

(Driving Forces)   *(Restraining Forces)*

———————————>< ———————————

———————————>< ———————————

———————————>< ———————————

———————————>< ———————————

———————————>< ———————————

———————————>< ———————————

———————————>< ———————————

TASK/RESPONSIBILITY MATRIX

	RESPONSIBILITY						
TASK							

P = Primary responsibility   S = Secondary responsibility   C = Communication loop

ACTION PLAN

ACTION STEP/ TASK	RESPONSIBLE PERSON/TEAM	BEGIN DATE	END DATE	EST. HOURS	EST. COST

THE PRACTICAL GUIDEBOOK COLLECTION
FROM RICHARD CHANG ASSOCIATES, INC.
PUBLICATIONS DIVISION

Our Practical Guidebook Collection is growing to meet the challenges of the ever-changing workplace of the 90's. Look for these and other titles from Richard Chang Associates, Inc. on your bookstore shelves and in book catalogs.

QUALITY IMPROVEMENT SERIES

- Meetings That Work!
- Continuous Improvement Tools Volume 1
- Continuous Improvement Tools Volume 2
- Step-By-Step Problem Solving
- Satisfying Internal Customers First!
- Continuous Process Improvement
- Improving Through Benchmarking
- Succeeding As A Self-Managed Team
- Reengineering In Action

MANAGEMENT SKILLS SERIES

- Coaching Through Effective Feedback
- Expanding Leadership Impact
- Mastering Change Management
- On-The-Job Orientation And Training
- Recreating Teams During Transitions

HIGH PERFORMANCE TEAM SERIES

- Success Through Teamwork
- Team Decision-Making Techniques
- Measuring Team Performance
- Building A Dynamic Team

HIGH-IMPACT TRAINING SERIES

- Creating High-Impact Training
- Identifying Targeted Training Needs
- Applying Successful Training Techniques
- Measuring The Impact Of Training
- Make Your Training Results Last

ADDITIONAL RESOURCES
FROM RICHARD CHANG ASSOCIATES, INC.

Improve your training sessions and seminars with the ideal tools—videos from Richard Chang Associates, Inc. You and your team will easily relate to the portrayals of real-life workplace situations. You can apply our innovative techniques to your own situations for immediate results.

TRAINING VIDEOTAPES

Mastering Change Management*
Turning Obstacles Into Opportunities

Step-By-Step Problem Solving*
A Practical Approach To Solving Problems On The Job

Quality: You Don't Have To Be Sick To Get Better**
Individuals Do Make a Difference

Achieving Results Through Quality Improvement**

*Authored by Dr. Richard Chang and produced by Double Vision Studios.
**Produced by American Media Inc. in conjunction with Richard Chang Associates, Inc.
  Each video includes a Facilitator's Guide.

"THE HUMAN EDGE SERIES" VIDEOTAPES

Total Quality: Myths, Methods, Or Miracles
Featuring Drs. Ken Blanchard and Richard Chang

Empowering The Quality Effort
Featuring Drs. Ken Blanchard and Richard Chang

Produced by Double Vision Studios.

"THE TOTAL QUALITY SERIES"
TRAINING VIDEOTAPES AND WORKBOOKS

Building Commitment *(Telly Award Winner)*
How To Build Greater Commitment To Your TQ Efforts

Teaming Up
How To Successfully Participate On Quality-Improvement Teams

Applied Problem Solving
How To Solve Problems As An Individual Or On A Team

Self-Directed Evaluation
How To Establish Feedback Methods To Self-Monitor Improvements

Authored by Dr. Richard Chang and produced by Double Vision Studios, each videotape from *"The Total Quality Series"* includes a *Facilitator's Guide* and five *Participant Workbooks* with each purchase. Additional *Participant Workbooks* are available for purchase.

EVALUATION AND FEEDBACK FORM

We need your help to continuously improve the quality of the resources provided through the Richard Chang Associates, Inc., Publications Division. We would greatly appreciate your input and suggestions regarding this particular guidebook, as well as future guidebook interests.

Please photocopy this form before completing it, since other readers may use this guidebook. Thank you in advance for your feedback.

Guidebook Title: _____

1. Overall, how would you rate your *level of satisfaction* with this guidebook? Please circle your response.

   Extremely Dissatisfied   Satisfied   Extremely Satisfied

   1   2   3   4   5

2. What specific *concepts or methods* did you find <u>most</u> helpful?

   _____
   _____

3. What specific *concepts or methods* did you find <u>least</u> helpful?

   _____
   _____

4. As an individual who may purchase additional guidebooks in the future, what *characteristics/features/benefits* are most important to you in making a decision to purchase a guidebook *(or another similar book)*?

   _____
   _____

5. What additional *subject matter/topic areas* would you like to see available as a guidebook in the future?

   _____
   _____

Name *(optional)*:_____

Address: _____

C/S/Z: _____   **Phone** ( ) _____